Original title:
A Dream Yet Awakened

Copyright © 2025 Swan Charm
All rights reserved.

Author: Eliora Lumiste
ISBN HARDBACK: 978-9908-1-4171-8
ISBN PAPERBACK: 978-9908-1-4172-5
ISBN EBOOK: 978-9908-1-4173-2

Dreams at the Edge of Day

Whispers of dawn in the quiet air,
Colors gleam softly, a lovely affair.
Shadows retreat as the light takes its claim,
Awakening hopes, igniting the flame.

Dreams at the Edge of Day

In fields full of blossoms, where wishes reside,
The heart finds its rhythm, with dreams as the guide.
Flowing like rivers, our visions expand,
Carried by breezes, a gentle command.

Dreams at the Edge of Day

Whirling in starlight, the night softly fades,
Mirroring moments that time never trades.
With each step we take on the path of our own,
We dance with the echoes, the seeds we have sown.

Dreams at the Edge of Day

Through glimmers of sunlight, we gather our tune,
In symphonies woven, like flowers in bloom.
The canvas of morning invites us to play,
As dreams stretch their wings at the edge of the day.

Dreams at the Edge of Day

So cherish the minutes, the magic we find,
In layers of beauty that soften the mind.
With wonder ablaze, let our spirits unfurl,
For dreams at the edge hold the heart of the world.

Glimmers of the Elusive

In twilight's soft embrace, they dance,
Whispers of dreams in a fleeting glance.
Flickers of light in shadows cast,
Moments remembered, but never grasped.

A breeze carries secrets through the night,
Echoes of wishes that take their flight.
Illusions shimmer like stars above,
Chasing the mysteries we dream of.

The Fragrance of Unlived Lives

In gardens where hopes are left to fade,
Petals of glory in silence laid.
Essence of dreams that never bloomed,
A tapestry woven in shadows groomed.

Whispers of laughter in echoes lost,
Unclaimed joys lingering, a heavy cost.
Fragrant memories in twilight's glow,
Yearning for paths we never know.

Starlit Paths Yet Traveled

Beneath the canvas of endless skies,
Footsteps echo where stardust lies.
Promise of journeys in silver threads,
Carried by dreams where adventure spreads.

Maps created by hearts yet unbound,
In the silence, new stories found.
The weight of the cosmos calls us near,
To explore the unknown without fear.

The Heartbeat of Horizon's Edge

Where sky kisses land with a gentle sigh,
The heartbeat of earth whispers, 'try.'
A rhythm that pulses in every wave,
Inviting the souls who dare to brave.

In the gold of dawn, dreams ignite,
Carving tales in the soft morning light.
The horizon beckons, a siren's call,
To chase the horizon, to risk it all.

Tides of the Unimagined

In whispers soft, the ocean sways,
The moonlight dances, casting rays.
Dreams unfurl on liquid grace,
As shadows drift in a timeless space.

Waves crash gently, secrets weave,
Stories born of what we believe.
Ever flowing, hearts expand,
As we reach for the unseen land.

With each pulse, new worlds ignite,
In the depths where dreams take flight.
Colors blend in a swirling tide,
Embracing all that we confide.

Ebb and flow, a rhythmic rhyme,
Carried forward through space and time.
Infinite realms just out of sight,
Awaiting hearts to seek the light.

So let the currents pull you near,
To realms of wonder, void of fear.
Explore the dreams the tides bestow,
In the vastness where visions glow.

Awakening the Hidden Realms

In shadows deep, the silence sighs,
Beneath the earth where magic lies.
A gentle spark ignites the night,
As mysteries unfold in flight.

Each rustling leaf, a tale unsung,
In whispered tones, the world is spun.
Through tangled roots and hidden ways,
Awakened dreams begin to blaze.

The heartbeat of the earth resounds,
In secret paths, where love abounds.
With open hearts, we start to see,
The realms where souls can roam so free.

In twilight's kiss, we find our voice,
Unraveling layers, we rejoice.
In the quiet where echoes dwell,
The hidden truths begin to swell.

So venture forth into the night,
Where every shadow holds a light.
Embrace the wonder, dive within,
To awaken realms where we begin.

Beneath the Surface of Sleep

In the quiet cradle of the night,
Where dreams take shape in soft twilight.
Sweet echoes of the day now fade,
As slumber's spell begins to invade.

Cascading thoughts like gentle streams,
Flow through the silence, weave our dreams.
With every breath, we drift away,
To realms where night and day betray.

Beneath the surface, thoughts may stir,
Whispers of hopes begin to blur.
Illusions dance in shadows deep,
As we awake from fragile sleep.

Voices linger, soft and sound,
In this stillness, peace is found.
We float on clouds, our fears unfurl,
In the embrace of a dreaming world.

So let the night enfold your heart,
And from the waking world depart.
Embrace the magic of the deep,
Beneath the surface of our sleep.

Chasing the Elusive Mirage

In deserts vast, where dreams are born,
The sun ignites, the earth is worn.
Mirages dance upon the sand,
Teasing hopes held in our hand.

With weary feet, we wander far,
Guided only by a distant star.
The winds may shift, the paths may change,
But still our hearts are free, unchained.

Every step, a quest for more,
Chasing shadows along the shore.
The fleeting glimpse of what might be,
Drives us forth on a journey free.

In the heat, our visions blur,
Yet still we chase, the dreams confer.
With courage deep, we push along,
Through illusions where we belong.

So take a breath, embrace the chase,
For every journey shapes our place.
In every mirage, a truth so bold,
Chasing dreams worth their weight in gold.

Reflections of an Untold Journey

In shadows deep, the path unfolds,
With dreams and fears, the tale retold.
Each step a whisper, softly worn,
The echoes linger, hopes reborn.

Through valleys low, the spirit soars,
As twilight hugs the closing doors.
With strength we carry, hearts ablaze,
In silence found, a thousand ways.

The rivers flow, their secrets keep,
While mountains watch us boldly leap.
In every gaze, a story bright,
Illuminates the coming night.

With every heartbeat, courage swells,
In whispers shared, the journey dwells.
An untold journey forged in grace,
Reflects the hope within our face.

Embers of the Unmanifested

In twilight's glow, ideas smolder,
Untamed sparks, our visions bolder.
Whispers dance on winds of chance,
Igniting dreams in fervent trance.

The canvas waits, a story bare,
With hues unseen, hearts laid bare.
From ashes rise, new worlds take flight,
Embers glow in the velvet night.

Each flicker holds a tale untold,
A spark of life, both brave and bold.
In silence, truths begin to form,
From nothingness, all art is born.

Through time and space, the visions weave,
A tapestry for those who believe.
In shadows cast, new paths abide,
Embers roar; ignited, we stride.

A Symphony of Colliding Realities

In layers deep, the worlds converge,
With vibrant tones, the thoughts emerge.
A symphony of life unfolds,
In every breath, a truth that holds.

Melodies clash, yet harmonize,
As echoes play beneath the skies.
In fractured light, reflections gleam,
Colliding paths, a wild dream.

Rhythms pulse in steady beat,
The essence felt beneath our feet.
In chaos found, the beauty thrives,
A dance of souls, where magic dives.

Between the notes, the silence breathes,
In hidden spaces, heart belief weaves.
As realms entwine, the story sways,
In this grand play, our spirits blaze.

Whispers of the Uncharted

Beyond the maps, the whispers call,
To wanderers who crave it all.
In shadowed realms, the secrets stir,
In quiet nights, the dreams confer.

Unseen paths where few have tread,
With every choice, the heart is led.
In echoes soft, the future breathes,
Embracing moments, the soul weaves.

With eyes attuned to subtle signs,
The universe in silence shines.
In uncharted lands, the courage grows,
As unknown tales begin to flow.

In journeys vast, the heart ignites,
With every step, a new delight.
Whispers guide through mist and haze,
In the uncharted, we find our ways.

Footprints in the Ethereal Sand

On shores where time is still,
We wander through the mist,
Barefoot on the cosmos' edge,
Our dreams are gently kissed.

Each step a whispered tale,
Carried by the ocean's sigh,
Footprints fade in twilight's glow,
As day and night comply.

The sand holds all our laughter,
Each grain a memory spun,
A journey through the heavens,
Beneath a setting sun.

Here, love's warmth embraces us,
In patterns soft and grand,
In every breeze that flutters by,
We leave our mark on sand.

So let us trace our stories,
Together hand in hand,
In this ethereal moment,
We walk the mystic land.

The Intersection of Dreams and Dawn

A world where shadows twinkle,
As night begins to break,
Between the realm of slumber,
And each new day we make.

The dreams weave bright narratives,
With whispers soft and clear,
In the stillness of the morn,
Awakening our fear.

The golden hues of sunrise,
Brush skies with gentle hands,
They meet the stars we cherished,
In twilight's fleeting bands.

Every hope, every longing,
Is captured in this light,
Where dawn meets soft illusions,
And dreams embrace the night.

So rise with open hearts,
And greet the sun's warm glow,
At the intersection of dreams,
Let our spirits flow.

Glances Back at Starlit Memories

In the tapestry of night,
I gaze at distant stars,
Each twinkle holds a story,
Of love that bears no scars.

Remembering the laughter,
Underneath the moon's embrace,
In the silence we were poets,
Of time and boundless space.

Every glance back reveals,
The echoes of our song,
In shadows soft and tender,
Where hearts will always belong.

Starlit paths we traveled,
In dreams that felt so vast,
With every wish that sparkled,
The present meets the past.

So let us hold those moments,
As constellations gleam,
In the night's gentle cradle,
We dance within a dream.

Whims of the Night's Canvas

The night unfolds its wonders,
A canvas deep and wide,
With shades of quiet whispers,
And stars that gleam with pride.

Each breeze a brush of magic,
Painting tales in the air,
With colors rich and vibrant,
That float beyond compare.

Moonlight spills its silver,
Across the darkened land,
Creating paths of wonder,
Tracing dreams with gentle hand.

Through shadows, secrets linger,
In silence, stories weave,
The night holds all our wishes,
For those who dare believe.

So let us dance in wonder,
Upon the night's embrace,
Where whimsy paints our journey,
In this enchanted space.

Canvas of Unseen Dreams

In shadows deep where colors blend,
A canvas waits for dreams to send.
Brushes dipped in midnight hues,
Create a world where visions choose.

A palette rich with hopes and fears,
Each stroke unveils the silent years.
Starlit whispers in the night,
Paint a tale of lost delight.

With every layer, secrets rise,
Imagined realms beneath the skies.
The heart's desire, bold and bright,
Rests on the edge of soft twilight.

Infinite stories on this space,
Each brush a chance to leave a trace.
In dreams we travel, hearts aglow,
A journey where the wild winds blow.

Here in the quiet, dreams take flight,
A world reborn in silver light.
The canvas waits, so fresh, so new,
For dreams unseen to come to view.

Whispers of Untraveled Landscapes

Beyond the hills, where shadows play,
Untraveled paths invite the day.
The whispering winds sing soft and low,
Of lands where only dreamers go.

Amber fields and skies of blue,
Hold secrets known to just a few.
Each step forward draws me near,
To ancient echoes, sweet and clear.

Mountains rise with tales to tell,
Of time entwined in nature's spell.
Rivers dance with silver streams,
Carrying the weight of dreams.

Through valleys lush, my heart will roam,
Finding solace away from home.
The beauty found in every glance,
Entices me to take a chance.

In whispers soft, the worlds invite,
To wander freely, hearts alight.
The untraveled calls, a siren's song,
Where every soul, at last, belongs.

The Veil Between Sleep and Reality

A realm awakes where shadows blend,
In gentle folds, where dreams descend.
The veil is thin, a gossamer thread,
Connecting worlds where few have tread.

Soft whispers glide on the edge of night,
Each fleeting thought a spark of light.
Between the realms, the magic sways,
In twilight's dance, where silence plays.

Moments linger, a heart's reprise,
As time collapses, truth defies.
Dreams arise in forms unknown,
A fragile space where seeds are sown.

The sigh of night, a lover's call,
Invites the wanderers to fall.
In slumber's grasp, reality bends,
As life and dreams become close friends.

To linger long in this sweet grace,
A canvas painted with each face.
Between the sleep and waking sound,
The secrets of the heart are found.

In the Embrace of Possibility

In quiet moments, stillness waits,
A door ajar, where chance creates.
Possibility dances on the breeze,
Inviting dreams with gentle ease.

Each heartbeat whispers, take the step,
To weave a tale that dreams can prep.
The world unfolds, a map of stars,
Guiding souls to rise from scars.

Within the unknown, sparks ignite,
Turning shadows into light.
With every breath, the magic grows,
In every choice, the journey flows.

The heart beats strong, a tethered song,
In the embrace where we belong.
Unfurl your wings, let courage soar,
There's endless wonder to explore.

In the embrace of what could be,
Life's canvas waits for you and me.
With open arms, we take the chance,
To live and love, to laugh, to dance.

The Awakening Dawn's Whisper

The sun peeks through the trees,
Awakening the sleepy skies,
Birds begin their morning song,
Nature stirs, as eyelids rise.

The gentle breeze begins to dance,
Rustling leaves in soft embrace,
Promises of warmth and light,
In this tranquil, sacred space.

Colors bloom in golden hues,
Painting shadows on the ground,
Life renews with every breath,
In the stillness, joy is found.

The world awakens, bold and bright,
Chasing dreams with every ray,
The dawn whispers of hope anew,
Guiding hearts along the way.

In this moment, time stands still,
As the day begins to glow,
Whispers echo through the air,
In the light, our spirits flow.

Notes from the World Beyond

Softly the echoes call to me,
Through the veil of dreams I roam,
A symphony of distant sighs,
Whispers of a place called home.

In shadows deep, the secrets lie,
Faint impressions in the night,
Messages from those who've flown,
Guiding spirits, sharing light.

Each note a thread that weaves the past,
In the tapestry of dreams,
Colors blend to form the song,
Of laughter, joy, and quiet beams.

Listen close, the world beyond,
Hums a tune of endless grace,
With every heartbeat, they remind,
Love endures in timeless space.

Between the realms, connection shows,
In every tear and every smile,
Notes that bridge the gap of time,
Resonate through every mile.

Shadows Resounding in the Heart

In corners dark where echoes dwell,
Shadows whisper tales untold,
Of dreams once bright that lost their light,
In the silence, fears unfold.

Yet from the depths, a spark ignites,
Hope's gentle flame begins to glow,
Each heartbeat thrums with life anew,
Resonating through the low.

Through shadows cast, we find the way,
Guided by an inner star,
Learning strength in darkest times,
Through struggles, we have traveled far.

In the heart's embrace, we stand,
Understanding blooms in quiet grace,
Shadows lend their bittersweet,
A reminder of our place.

As echoes fade into the night,
We rise with courage, sharp and clear,
For shadows may resound in us,
But love will always persevere.

The Light Beyond the Fog

Mist enfolds the quiet morn,
Veiling paths in silver shrouds,
Yet whispers beckon from afar,
A promise hiding in the clouds.

Through the haze, a flicker glows,
Gentle warmth against the chill,
A beacon calls with every breath,
Stirring hope, igniting will.

The fog may cling, but spirits rise,
Chasing shadows with each stride,
For in the depth of nature's breath,
The light becomes our faithful guide.

As daybreak harshly parts the veil,
Light cascades in vibrant streams,
Once lost in doubt, now found in grace,
Revealing all our brightest dreams.

So let the morning lead us forth,
Stepping boldly, hearts aglow,
For light awaits beyond the fog,
And love will light the path we go.

Awakened Horizons

The sun breaks through the veil of night,
A canvas painted soft and bright.
Birds stretch their wings, embrace the sky,
In this moment, dreams learn to fly.

Mountains whisper tales of old,
Their secrets wrapped in hues of gold.
Rivers dance, with laughter clear,
As nature beckons, drawing near.

Fields of flowers bow and sway,
In gentle winds, they find their way.
Colors blend, a vibrant throng,
An endless chorus, nature's song.

Voices echo, hope's refrain,
In every drop of falling rain.
The world awakens, fresh and new,
Each moment holds a mystic view.

Awakened hearts, arise with grace,
To embrace the dawn's warm embrace.
In every breath, the promise glows,
Of horizons vast, where wonder flows.

The Stillness Between Thoughts

In quietude where whispers dwell,
A sacred space, where dreams compel.
The mind finds warmth in gentle pause,
Awakening beauty, without cause.

Moments linger, soft and clear,
Silent echoes, drawing near.
In the stillness, we discern,
The subtle flames of passion burn.

Thoughts like ripples on a stream,
Fleeting figures, lost in a dream.
Yet in this hush, we find our core,
The heart's soft fervor, wanting more.

Each breath a melody, sweet and light,
A dance of shadows, hinting bright.
In between, the silence sings,
Of life's sweet whispers, fragile wings.

Here we gather, souls align,
In the stillness, love will shine.
Embracing what the heart has sought,
In quietude, solace is wrought.

Liminal Spaces and Eternal Yearning

In the crack between dusk and dawn,
Dreams linger softly, never gone.
Unraveled threads of hope and light,
In liminal shades, we take our flight.

Moments fleeting, caught in time,
A dance of echoes, steeped in rhyme.
Where shadows meet the dawn's first gleam,
Our hearts ignite, fueled by the dream.

Eternal yearning whispers low,
Through winding paths, we yearn to go.
In every pause, a truth unfolds,
A gentle longing, brave and bold.

In twilight's embrace, we intertwine,
Fingers brushing, fate's design.
The air alive with unspoken cheer,
In these spaces, we shed our fear.

Through darkened lands, we wander free,
Chasing the stars, a tapestry.
In liminal realms, we craft our fate,
With hearts ablaze, we navigate.

A Mosaic of Unexplored Echoes

In hidden corners, whispers weave,
A tapestry of what we believe.
Echoes dance on the edge of thought,
In silence, the unspoken is sought.

Each fragment glimmers, bright and rare,
A mosaic of dreams laid bare.
Colors clash and gently merge,
In every pulse, a vibrant surge.

From shadows cast by fear and doubt,
Emerges light, a joyful shout.
In every heart, a story waits,
To break the chains and open gates.

Beneath the surface, longing flows,
In unexplored echoes, love bestows.
A symphony of souls entwined,
In every moment, truth we find.

Together we build, piece by piece,
A world where fears can find release.
In this mosaic, dreams take flight,
Unexplored echoes shine so bright.

The Call of the Unexplored

Beyond the hills where shadows play,
A whisper beckons, drawing me near.
Forgotten trails in the light of day,
Adventure calls, I feel no fear.

The winding paths, a silent song,
Each step I take, my spirit soars.
In lands where I know I belong,
Discovery waits behind closed doors.

Nature's brush paints skies of gold,
With every dawn, a brand new start.
A tale of courage waiting to unfold,
In uncharted realms, I play my part.

The stars above, they twinkle bright,
Guiding the way through night so deep.
With every heartbeat, pure delight,
Into the wild, my dreams I keep.

Step lightly now, toward the unknown,
For every journey begins with a sigh.
The call of the unexplored is shown,
In every breath, I long to fly.

Portals of the Unfathomable

Beyond the veil where secrets dwell,
A shimmering door awaits my gaze.
With whispered truths, it casts a spell,
To take me where the mind can blaze.

In twilight's grace, the shadows dance,
A flicker of light in endless night.
Through portals vast, I dare to chance,
The depths of dreams, a wondrous sight.

Dimensions twist in colors bright,
Each world a gem yet to be seen.
In cosmic waves, I find my light,
Through realms where I become the keen.

The unfathomable calls to me,
Its language woven, deep like time.
Within its grasp, I am set free,
A soul unbound, a spirit prime.

As stars align and worlds collide,
I hear the echoes of the lost.
Through portals wide, I must decide,
Embrace the journey, pay the cost.

Where Wishes Gently Rest

In quiet corners of the heart,
Where dreams linger, soft and bright.
Wishes painted like fine art,
In twilight's hush, they take their flight.

Beneath the stars, a tender sigh,
In silver pools of moonlit glow.
Each hope a feather, yearning high,
To touch the skies, to ride the flow.

With every breath, the whispers bloom,
In gardens rich with fragrant grace.
Where wishes rest and love finds room,
In gentle arms, a warm embrace.

The world may spin, yet here I stay,
Where dreams are cherished, held so dear.
In secret folds, I weave my way,
To find the magic hidden near.

So here I close my eyes and dream,
In tranquil realms, my heart confessed.
For every thought, a radiant beam,
In the quiet nook where wishes rest.

The Dance of Forgotten Seasons

In autumn's glow, the leaves take flight,
A tapestry of gold and red.
Whispers of summer, fading light,
In memories where dreams are spread.

The winter snow, a silent shroud,
Cradles the earth in purest white.
In stillness, nature's beauty loud,
Each frosted branch a twinkling sight.

Then spring awakens with its song,
Petals unfurl in joyful grace.
The dance goes on, it won't be long,
As life returns in warm embrace.

And summer comes with fiery sun,
The days expand, the laughter flows.
Each season's tale, a story spun,
In circles where the river goes.

The dance of time, a constant show,
With every turn, a chance to change.
In every heartbeat, love will grow,
Through seasons past, forever strange.

Echoes Along the Crossroads

Whispers linger in the air,
Paths diverge, with stories rare.
Footsteps echo on the ground,
In the silence, wisdom found.

Figures dance in twilight's glow,
Choices made, the heart will show.
Fates entwined like branches twined,
At the crossroads, truth aligned.

Shadows stretch as dusk descends,
Time holds tight but never bends.
With each step, the echoes blend,
In this place where journeys end.

Voices call from paths unseen,
Limitless in what they mean.
Holding dreams within our hands,
Guided by the unseen strands.

In the twilight, futures shift,
Every choice a precious gift.
Echoes fade but always stay,
Lighting up the darkest way.

Hidden Pathways of the Night

Starry skies conceal the trails,
Winding paths where silence hails.
Mysterious whispers softly speak,
In the shadows, visions peek.

Moonlight filters through the trees,
Gentle winds carry secrets, please.
Footfalls quiet on the ground,
Lost in dreams where hope is found.

Wanderers seek what lies ahead,
Mapping routes where others tread.
In the dark, the heart can find,
Threads of fate that are entwined.

Every twist holds stories old,
Courage blooms in paths so bold.
In the night's embrace, we roam,
Finding solace far from home.

Through the hush, a spark ignites,
Guiding souls to wondrous sights.
Hidden pathways beckon near,
Leading hearts without a fear.

The Breath Between Moments

In the pause, the world holds sway,
Life suspended, dreams at play.
Every heartbeat whispers truth,
Silent echoes of our youth.

Caught between the now and then,
Glimmers of what could have been.
In the quiet, time stands still,
Moments captured, felt at will.

Gentle sighs in twilight hues,
Breaths of life in shades of blues.
Fragments linger, soft and sweet,
In the stillness, we retreat.

The spaces hold our hopes and fears,
Timeless whispers through the years.
Each second blooms like fragile flowers,
In the breath, we find the hours.

Suspend the rush, embrace the grace,
Find your time, your sacred space.
In the hush, we come alive,
Learning how to truly thrive.

Ephemeral Connections

Fleeting touches, soft as air,
Moments woven with great care.
In the blink, hearts intertwine,
Ephemeral yet so divine.

Brief encounters light the soul,
Each connection plays its role.
Whispers shared, like fleeting dreams,
Lingers sweet in sunlit beams.

Paths cross lightly, then depart,
Leaving traces on the heart.
In the echoes of what's past,
We find meanings that will last.

Every smile, a spark ignites,
Binding souls on starry nights.
Life unfolds in gentle ways,
In the dance of passing days.

Cherish each ephemeral thread,
Memories of words unsaid.
In these moments, love reflects,
Life's deep beauty, it connects.

Secrets in the Silent Hours

Whispers blend with shadows deep,
Echoes of the secrets we keep.
Moonlight casts its gentle glow,
Silent thoughts begin to flow.

In this realm where dreams take flight,
Hidden truths come into sight.
Winds of change softly call,
In the night, we lose it all.

Stars above begin to gleam,
Fading in a distant dream.
Memories drift like autumn leaves,
In stillness, the heart believes.

Time dissolves in the cool air,
Moments lost, forever rare.
As the night bends to our will,
Secrets in the silence thrill.

Tales of love, of loss, of grace,
In these hours, we find our place.
Where shadows dance and linger long,
In silent hours, we are strong.

Threads of a Faded Vision

Frayed edges of a distant dream,
Whispers woven in a seam.
Colors fade, yet stories stay,
Threads of time, they drift away.

In the fabric of our fate,
Old visions, though they wait.
Patterns shifting, lives entwined,
In each thread, a truth defined.

Hues of joy and shades of pain,
Craft our stories, love and gain.
Through the distance, we still see,
Threads that bind you close to me.

Echoes linger in every stitch,
Moments shared, both rich and rich.
Faded visions may distort,
But in our hearts, they still report.

Gentle hands that weave and mend,
Faded patterns, yet they bend.
In such threads, our lives align,
Woven dreams, forever shine.

Half-Lit Pathways

Underneath the moon's soft gaze,
Half-lit pathways lead through haze.
Steps uncertain, but still strong,
Guided by a distant song.

Footprints left in twilight's glow,
Stories whispered, winds that blow.
In the shadows, truths reveal,
Half-lit paths that softly heal.

Courage found in murky nights,
Flickers of our inner lights.
Through the branches, stars peak through,
Half-lit pathways, dreams renew.

Every turn a chance to grow,
In the dark, we come to know.
That in stillness, hope ignites,
Half-lit pathways, peace invites.

Journey on, let spirits soar,
In the half-light, we explore.
Leading us to brighter days,
Where love and light always stays.

When the Night Sings Softly

When the night sings softly sweet,
Crickets play a warm retreat.
Moonbeams dance on rooftops high,
Dreams awaken with a sigh.

Melodies of stars align,
In the dark, our hearts entwine.
Every note, a gentle kiss,
In the night, we find our bliss.

Whispered hopes float on the air,
With each breath, a tender prayer.
As the shadows start to weave,
In the night, we dare believe.

Softly, secrets shared in trust,
In the night, it's more than just.
As the stillness swells around,
In each heartbeat, love is found.

So let the night embrace our souls,
As it sings, it gently pulls.
In the quiet, we are free,
When the night sings, you and me.

Songs of the Unfinished

Whispers of dreams lie in shadows,
Dancing on edges of time's flow.
Each echo speaks of paths untaken,
A melody of what could be shown.

Ink spills on pages, thoughts take flight,
Crafting tales in dim candlelight.
Unraveled stories still to explore,
Leaving hearts hungry for more.

In the silence, hopes gently stir,
Filling the void with sweet murmurs.
A symphony waits in every sigh,
As the unfinished yearns to fly.

Beneath the stars, our visions blend,
Weaving beginnings that never end.
Each note a promise yet to be sung,
In the realm where the unsung belong.

Embrace the journey, let it unfold,
For in the unfinished, treasures are told.
With every heartbeat, a chance to ignite,
The songs of the unfinished ignite the night.

The Heart of Serendipity

In the tapestry of chance, we find,
Moments woven, threads intertwined.
A smile exchanged on a bustling street,
Destinies collide, strangers meet.

Every turn holds a hidden grace,
Life's surprises, a warm embrace.
Unexpected blessings shining bright,
Guiding us softly into the light.

Whispers of fate, they softly beckon,
In the chaos, sweet truth reckons.
Finding joy in the simplest things,
This is the song that serendipity sings.

With open hearts, let us explore,
The beauty in what life has in store.
Uncharted paths, where wonders reside,
In the heart of serendipity, we confide.

Through tangled roots, we shall roam,
Building stories, finding a home.
In the dance of fate, we come alive,
For in serendipity, we truly thrive.

Tides of the Unimagined

Waves roll in with stories untold,
Currents of dreams, both timid and bold.
The shores of tomorrow whisper and sigh,
Carrying wishes on a seagull's cry.

In twilight's glow, horizons expand,
Navigating worlds crafted by hand.
Unseen treasures lie beneath the foam,
The tides of the unimagined call us home.

With each ebb, a mystery born,
A canvas of night, a promise of dawn.
We cast our nets into the unknown,
Hoping to find what the heart has sown.

Let the winds guide our curious sails,
Through uncharted seas where adventure prevails.
In the salty air, possibilities dance,
The tides of the unimagined offer a chance.

Together we'll wander, wild and free,
Chasing the tales of what's yet to be.
In every wave, a new chance to see,
The beauty of life in its mystery.

Flickering Lanterns of Tomorrow

In the night, hopes twinkle bright,
Lanterns flicker, casting soft light.
Each glow holds dreams waiting to rise,
Guiding us gently beneath starry skies.

With fragile flames, we chart our course,
Harnessing fears, we tap into force.
Tales of tomorrow dance in the air,
A symphony rich, woven with care.

As shadows play, our spirits ignite,
In the warmth of togetherness, we unite.
The future whispers, vacant and wide,
Flickering lanterns, our steady guide.

Through valleys of doubt and mountains of cheer,
We forge connections, so precious and dear.
With every lantern, a vision we claim,
Together we rise, kindling hope's flame.

So lift your lantern, let it soar,
For tomorrow awaits on the far shore.
In the dance of twilight, we gleam and glow,
Flickering lanterns, the paths we will go.

Murmurs of the Midnight Muse

Under the veil of night,
Whispers weave through the trees.
Softly calling, dreams take flight,
Carried on the evening breeze.

Shadows flutter, spirits play,
As the moon begins to rise.
Echoes of the past drift away,
Painting tales in silver skies.

Stars collide in silent bliss,
Moments captured, fleeting chance.
In the dark, we find our kiss,
Lost within the midnight dance.

Gentle sighs and secret words,
Embers glow in fading light.
Thoughts take shape like startled birds,
Free to roam in velvet night.

Here within this mystic space,
Muses hum their haunting tune.
In their arms, I find my place,
Cradled by the watchful moon.

Chasing Distant Stars

In the quiet of the night,
Dreamers chase what eyes can't see.
Guided by the stars so bright,
Hearts aflame, we wander free.

Through the dark, a path unfolds,
Glowing gems in endless sky.
Stories whispered, secrets told,
In the cosmos, spirits fly.

With each pulse of starlit fire,
Hope ignites in soft embrace.
Chasing dreams, we climb higher,
Finding solace in this space.

Every twinkle a sweet sign,
Promises of what could be.
Boundless love, our hearts align,
As we dance with destiny.

In the universe, we strive,
Fingers reaching for the light.
Together, we feel alive,
Chasing distant stars through night.

Fantasies in the Dawn

Awakening to the breeze,
Colors bloom in soft array.
Whispers of the waking trees,
Signal dawn of a new day.

Sunrise paints the world anew,
Golden rays on dewy grass.
Every dream feels bright and true,
Moments cherished, time must pass.

In the air, sweet scents arise,
Melodies on morning's breath.
Nature's art, a grand surprise,
Life anew escapes from death.

Dancing light on flowing streams,
Sparkling gems in sunlight's grace.
Filling hearts with tender dreams,
Time slows down, a soft embrace.

As the day unfolds its plan,
We step forth, a hopeful throng.
In each glance, the world can span,
Fantasies where we belong.

Where Shadows Dance Lightly

In the twilight's gentle glow,
Shadows stretch and softly sway.
Underneath the stars' soft show,
Nighttime sings what dreams convey.

Echoes lead through paths unknown,
Whispers float on evening air.
In this realm, we're not alone,
Magic twirls with tender care.

Silhouettes of memory,
Flickering like candlelight.
In their midst, we come to be,
Bound by dusk, we find delight.

Every heartbeat tells a tale,
Every breath a secret shared.
In the silence, dreams prevail,
Holding tight, we feel prepared.

As the night begins to pass,
Shadows wane but not in vain.
In each step, we find our class,
Dancing lightly, free from pain.

Fragments of a Fading Illusion

In whispers soft, dreams collide,
Echoes linger, nowhere to hide.
Fleeting shadows, fading light,
Hopes that shimmer, lost in night.

Time erodes the vibrant hues,
Memories tangled, paths to choose.
Each promise whispered in the dark,
Leaves behind a muted mark.

Glimmers tease in twilight's hand,
Shifting shapes in drifting sand.
What once felt solid fades away,
Leaving only shades of gray.

Fragments scattered, stories told,
Worn by years, silvered, bold.
A journey etched in fading lines,
Reveals the truth that time defines.

Yet in the silence, hope persists,
A fragile spark that still exists.
For even as the soul may fray,
A breath of dawn breaks through the gray.

The Unseen Horizon

A distant line, where sky meets land,
Promises linger, forever planned.
In dreams we chase, the sunlit view,
Yet paths unknown pull us anew.

Across the waves, the whispers play,
Guiding hearts in the light of day.
Beyond the reach of our tired sight,
The horizon waits, a call to flight.

With every step, the world expands,
Vast and wild, the touch of hands.
In every heartbeat, stories wait,
Future woven, destined fate.

Searching for the signs that gleam,
Reality dances, a fleeting dream.
Yet still we wander, a steadfast crew,
The unseen waits, with wonders true.

Each dawn arrives, a canvas bright,
Painting visions in morning light.
And though unseen, it's always near,
The horizon whispers, "Do not fear."

Shadows of Uncharted Desires

In corners dark, our wishes breathe,
Flickering flames beneath the sheath.
Desires pulsing like hidden streams,
Awakening long-forgotten dreams.

The shadows dance on the walls of night,
Carving paths in elusive light.
Each whispered hope, a fragile thread,
In uncharted lands, where none have tread.

With every heartbeat, secrets stir,
Yearnings echo, a quiet purr.
Drawing maps in the starry skies,
Crafting tales where the spirit flies.

Adventure calls through veils of mist,
Compelling wonders, too sweet to resist.
Yet still the shadows hold their sway,
Shaping desires in their own play.

Embrace the whispers, let them lead,
To realms where only dreams are freed.
For in each shadow, a spark remains,
A promise veiled, where hope sustains.

When Night Meets the Daylight

As twilight falls, the world transforms,
A dance of light in shifting forms.
Stars emerge in the fading blue,
Crescent moons greet the night anew.

When darkness wraps in soft embrace,
The day sighs low, a gentle grace.
Melding whispers, where borders blur,
Time's sweet passage stirs a purr.

With every breath, the magic swells,
In quiet tones, the heart compels.
When night slips in, with mysteries deep,
The world reveals its secret keep.

Colors shift in a lover's sigh,
Dreams ignite as the shadows fly.
Embracing night with open arms,
Awakening all its dormant charms.

And as the dawn begins to break,
A fragile peace we dare to take.
For when night meets the daylight's grace,
A timeless dance, a warm embrace.

Lullabies of the Unwritten

Whispers of dreams in the night,
Melodies soft, out of sight.
Hopes wrapped in shadows, they soar,
Gentle the night, forevermore.

Stars twinkle in skies so deep,
Secrets they guard, secrets they keep.
The moon sings softly, a sweet refrain,
Cradling wishes like drops of rain.

Silent stories on the breeze,
Carried along with tender ease.
Each note a wish, each sigh a plea,
In the embrace of eternity.

Visions dance in shimmering light,
Guiding the lost through the night.
In lullabies, our hearts take flight,
Dreamers awake in the fading twilight.

Unwritten tales that time unfurls,
Crafted by fate in secret whirls.
Lulled by the rhythm, we find our way,
In the hush of night, we gently sway.

Echoes of a Fractured Time

Fragments of moments drift like dust,
Memories cherished, but gone they must.
Time twists and bends, a fickle friend,
Echoes linger, never to mend.

Tick of the clock, a reminder clear,
Lost in the past, but still so near.
Whispers of yesteryear call aloud,
In the silence, a haunting shroud.

Veils of nostalgia cloak the heart,
Each echo a reminder, tearing apart.
Shattered reflections in whispered tones,
The fabric of time, woven in bones.

Shadows of laughter and pain collide,
In this fractured realm, where dreams reside.
We chase the moments, elusive and fleet,
Searching for solace, for time's retreat.

Time holds its secrets, both bitter and sweet,
Each echo a chance, a rhythmic heartbeat.
In the labyrinth of what used to be,
We find traces of our history.

Patches of Fading Light

Dappled sunlight through the trees,
Fading warmth carried by the breeze.
Whispers of dusk wrap the day,
Gentle hues that softly sway.

Shadows stretch with a tender grace,
Embers glow in a quiet space.
Patches of light in twilight's embrace,
Nature whispers, time finds its pace.

Colors bleed into the night,
Softened edges, a fading sight.
Moments captured in warm delight,
Holding on to the fading light.

A symphony of silence, profound,
Crickets sing while the stars surround.
In fading moments, solace found,
As daylight bows to night renowned.

Patches of light, where dreams reside,
In gentle hues, we find our guide.
With every glance, we seek the bright,
In fading hues of our shared night.

The Awakening Dusk

As day retreats, the sky ignites,
A canvas brushed with golden lights.
Silhouettes dance on the horizon's edge,
Whispers of twilight, a gentle pledge.

Colors meld in a vibrant blaze,
Awakening dusk in a soft embrace.
Beauty unfolds, both wild and free,
The day's last breath, a silent decree.

Stars peek through the velvet veil,
Glimmers of hope in a wondrous tale.
With every heartbeat, the world aligns,
In the glow of dusk, the spirit shines.

A symphony plays in the fading glow,
Echoes of nature, a steady flow.
In the hush of dusk, dreams intertwine,
Awakening hearts, the night divine.

As time drifts softly into the night,
We cherish the dusk, our hearts take flight.
In the awakening, we find our truth,
In twilight's embrace, the dance of youth.

Pages from a Lost Chronicle

In dusty tomes, the stories sleep,
Whispers of voices, secrets they keep.
Time's gentle hand has turned each page,
But still they linger, a silent sage.

Lost in the folds of memories gray,
Words weave a tapestry, night into day.
Heroes and lovers, battles once fought,
In ink and parchment, all lessons taught.

Echoes of laughter, shadows of tears,
Each line a journey through countless years.
Forgotten paths in a world so vast,
Yet within these pages, the future's cast.

Dust motes dance in the golden light,
Each stroke of pen, ignites the night.
A laughter recalled, a sorrow unveiled,
In chronicles lost, true dreams are jailed.

Who dares to read, to pen anew?
Awakening stories, both old and true.
Turn soft the pages, let them unfold,
For every lost tale is a treasure gold.

Sighs of the Unseen

Beneath the surface, where shadows play,
Whispers linger in the light of day.
The unseen sighs, like autumn leaves,
Carried by winds, as the heart believes.

Silent wishes on the breeze caught,
Echoes of dreams, the world forgot.
Within the silence, a vibrant pulse,
Each breath a story, a heart's convulse.

Glimmers of hope in the deepest night,
Flickering softly, a fleeting light.
Reach for the ether, let it reveal,
The sighs of the unseen, a truth to heal.

Invisible paths weave in the dark,
Choosing to follow, igniting a spark.
In the stillness, a dance so divine,
Connecting our souls, in every line.

Hear the whispers, let them intwine,
For in the unseen, our dreams align.
Through silent moments, we come alive,
In sighs of the unseen, we truly thrive.

Threads of Moonlit Wishes

Stitched in silver, the night is spun,
Threads of wishes, where dreams are begun.
In quiet corners of hearts that yearn,
Moonlit tales in the shadows burn.

Glimmers woven through velvet skies,
Potent wishes on whispered sighs.
Each star a mirror reflecting desires,
Bathed in magic, the soul aspires.

From distant shores where the oceans sigh,
Carries the echoes of a lullaby.
In every petal, in every breeze,
Lies the promise of what is to seize.

Fingers entwining, reaching for hope,
Under the spells where the dreamers cope.
Dance in the light of enchanted nights,
Celebrate life with its countless flights.

Mending our hearts with threads spun at dusk,
Embracing the moonlight, the dreamers' husk.
In the weave of the night, our wishes align,
Threads of moonlit wishes, eternally shine.

Awakening Within the Shadows

In folds of twilight where secrets breathe,
Awakening whispers the darkness weaves.
A tapestry woven with threads of gray,
Inviting the soul to dance and sway.

Beneath the quiet, a heartbeat pounds,
In silent realms, where freedom resounds.
Shadows embrace with an alluring grace,
A hidden world, a sacred space.

Glimmers of light pierce the night's cocoon,
Each moment a promise, a forgotten tune.
Embrace the void, let fears take flight,
Awakening dreams under starry light.

In the cradle of night, let spirits rise,
Casting aside the web of lies.
In darkness, we flourish, our truths reclaim,
Awakening within, igniting the flame.

Together we journey where shadows fall,
Unraveling myths, we heed the call.
From whispered echoes to radiant glow,
Awakening within, we blossom and grow.

The Unraveled Tapestry of Dreams

In the quiet night, whispers unfold,
Threads of desires and stories untold.
Woven with hope, yet frayed at the seams,
A tapestry bright, born from our dreams.

Colors fade softly, merging like thoughts,
Fragments of laughter and battles we fought.
With every unravel, a lesson defined,
In the fabric of life, our hearts intertwined.

Each pattern reveals a moment we shared,
Moments of joy, and times when we cared.
Yet shadows loom close, casting doubt on the glow,
The tapestry shifts, as we ebb and flow.

As fabric is torn, we strengthen our will,
Found in the chaos, a purpose to fill.
For dreams never perish, but endlessly weave,
A story that lives in the heart of believe.

So let us embrace each thread, every strand,
In the tapestry of dreams, together we stand.
The unending journey, the patterns we trace,
In the light of our hopes, we find our own place.

Sails of Unseen Seas

Upon the horizon, where daylight meets night,
Sails of unseen seas begin their flight.
Venturing forth, with the wind at our back,
Toward distant shores, from the familiar track.

With each wave's crest, adventure calls loud,
A dance with the ocean, wild and unbowed.
Secrets of water lie deep and profound,
In the silence of depths, lost treasures are found.

Stars above shimmer, like guides in the dark,
Their light casts a path, igniting a spark.
With courage our vessel, and dreams as our chart,
We sail on a journey that opens the heart.

The sails catch the whispers of tales yet to share,
Of islands of magic, and realms beyond care.
In the wind's gentle breath, our spirits take flight,
Sails of unseen seas, dancing with light.

As dawn paints the sky with colors anew,
We navigate waters, both fierce and so blue.
Each voyage a memory, each wave a new tale,
On the sails of unseen seas, we prevail.

Reflections in a Dreamlike Glass

In a world of whispers, where dreams take flight,
Reflections shimmer, bathed in soft light.
A glass that reveals, the heart's hidden layers,
Mirrored illusions of hopes and prayers.

Each glance shows a story, a moment, a truth,
Captured in silence, the essence of youth.
Ripples of memories dance in the mist,
In the dreamlike glass, not a moment is missed.

Faces appear, from the past, they collide,
Echoes of laughter, some joy, some cried.
Yet time bends in this realm with such grace,
In the quiet of dreams, we find our own place.

The glass holds reflections of what we hold dear,
Fragments of love, and whispers of fear.
Yet deep in its heart, a beauty so bold,
In the dreamlike glass, our stories unfold.

So gaze into depths where your soul can roam,
In reflections so vivid, you'll find your true home.
Shattered or whole, each piece plays its part,
In the dreamlike glass, lies the map of the heart.

Cascading Thoughts Beneath Starlight

Beneath starlit skies, thoughts start to cascade,
Gentle as whispers, a nocturnal parade.
Each twinkling light, a beacon of dreams,
Flowing like rivers, or soft flowing streams.

The moon casts a glow, on paths left behind,
Chasing reflections, both tender and kind.
In the silence of night, our worries take flight,
Cascading like stars, they vanish from sight.

Each thought like a petal in the cool night air,
Drifting and dancing, shedding our care.
From the depths of our minds, to the vastness above,
Cascading thoughts gathering, wrapped in pure love.

The cosmos our witness, embraces our souls,
In the blanket of night, where wildness unfolds.
We gather the moments, spun in silver thread,
Cascading reflections of everything said.

So beneath starlit dreams, let your spirit ignite,
In the cascade of thoughts, find your inner light.
For through the unknown, we journey and weave,
In the starlit embrace, we learn to believe.

The Canvas of Untold Journeys

Upon a stretch of endless skies,
Colors swirl where freedom flies.
Brushstrokes beckon, tales unfold,
Adventures waiting to be told.

Footprints mark the path unknown,
In every heart, a dream has grown.
With each step, a story we weave,
On this canvas, we believe.

Mountains rise and rivers bend,
Time is fleeting, journeys blend.
Every horizon calls our name,
In the quest, we find our flame.

Through storms we sail, through calm we glide,
Together, side by side we ride.
The canvas vast, the brush our own,
In every stroke, our lives are shown.

Whispers of the world around,
Every heartbeat, every sound.
Colors merge in wild array,
Tales of nights and dreams by day.

Shards of Light in Twilight

As day descends and shadows creep,
A world awakens from its sleep.
Stars emerge with gentle grace,
In twilight's arms, they find their place.

Whispers float on evening's breeze,
Echoes carried through the trees.
Glints of silver, pearls of light,
Illuminate the coming night.

Moments captured, fleeting glow,
In the dark, our spirits flow.
Between the worlds of day and night,
Shards of dreams take sudden flight.

A canvas painted soft and wide,
Where hope and memories collide.
Underneath the vast expanse,
Twilight grants our souls a chance.

Hold these fragments, keep them near,
In the silence, they are clear.
A dance of light, a quiet call,
In twilight's grasp, we find it all.

Voices from the Abyss of Dreams

In the depths where shadows dwell,
Whispers weave their ancient spell.
Voices call from realms afar,
Guiding souls like distant stars.

Dreams take flight on silken wings,
Circuitous paths that fate now brings.
In the dark, a lullaby,
A haunting tune beneath the sky.

Through the veil of midnight's breath,
Echoes dance with hints of death.
Yet in the void, we find our light,
Beneath the stars, we seek the night.

Fragments of the past still linger,
In every thought, a ghostly singer.
The abyss holds secrets prized,
In dreams uncharted, truth lies disguised.

Unravel tales in silent screams,
Awakened gently from our dreams.
The voices call, a siren's song,
In the abyss, we all belong.

The Paradox of Waking Worlds

In dawn's embrace, the shadows break,
Awake, we toss, begin to wake.
Reality bends, a twisted play,
In waking worlds, we lose our way.

Light cascades, yet darkness hides,
In open hearts, the contrast resides.
Moments blend, like day and night,
A paradox of wrong and right.

The mind's vast sea, a swirling thought,
In every drift, a lesson taught.
Awareness flickers, dims, and glows,
In waking realms, uncertainty flows.

We chase the dreams, yet wake anew,
In waking worlds, the strange feels true.
What seems unreal may just be real,
In this dance, our fate we seal.

Caught in cycles, round we go,
Chasing winds that whisper low.
In waking worlds, we search for peace,
In paradox, our journey's lease.

Whispers of the Unseen

Softly they speak in the night,
Echoes of dreams taking flight.
In shadows where secrets reside,
They dance where the whispers hide.

Fleeting, they weave through the air,
Gentle reminders of care.
In silence, they hold the key,
To truths only night can see.

Listen, the world sings low,
A lullaby only they know.
In the corners of stillness found,
Whispers murmur without sound.

Through curtains of mist, they sigh,
Promising not to say goodbye.
In twilight's gentle embrace,
They leave behind a trace.

To those who dare to believe,
In moments where spirits weave,
The unseen will always show,
Where the heart dares to go.

Echoes in Twilight's Embrace

In the dusk where dreams convene,
Shadows dance, serene, unseen.
Whispers float on the breeze,
Easing the heart, hearts at ease.

Colors melt in hues of night,
Stars awaken, pure delight.
Each echo tells a tale,
Of longing, love, and sail.

Beneath the veil of fading light,
Time suspends, holding tight.
Every breath a song sung low,
Guiding souls where they must go.

In twilight's calm, we must trust,
The echoes blend, the stardust.
With every step on paths unknown,
The heart finds a way back home.

Embraced by colors warm and bright,
In memories, we take flight.
The twilight's kiss, soft and pure,
Whispers promise, love will endure.

The Slumbering Horizon

Beyond the edge where day meets night,
A slumbering horizon takes flight.
Dreams weave through the gathering mist,
Where moments linger, softly kissed.

Glistening waves of amber hue,
Hold the hopes of mornings new.
With every heartbeat, they sigh,
Carrying whispers that fly.

Silhouettes of dreams arise,
As twilight paints the skies.
In the hush of the in-between,
The world breathes calm and serene.

Gentle shadows follow the sun,
In anticipation, they run.
To greet the dawn with open arms,
Where the heart finds endless charms.

In the distance, a promise glows,
Of paths unknown that life bestows.
For every day is a new embrace,
In the heart of the horizon's grace.

Visions Beyond the Veil

Beneath the stars, a secret sigh,
Visions awaken, spirits fly.
In the hush of the night's array,
Truths whisper and softly sway.

Through the veil of dreams, they wade,
Where light and shadow are made.
In twilight's grasp, they ignite,
Guiding souls through the night.

Reflections of what could be,
Shimmer in the eye's decree.
Each moment a chance to see,
Beyond the known, wild and free.

The dance of fate begins anew,
In vibrant hues, life's debut.
With every heartbeat, worlds unfold,
In the stories yet untold.

Embrace the visions, let them soar,
Beyond the veil, reach for more.
In silence, magic finds its way,
Guiding hearts in night's ballet.

Whispers of the Unconscious

In shadows deep where secrets lie,
The murmurs of the heart sigh low,
Hidden dreams begin to fly,
In twilight's glow, the thoughts will flow.

A tapestry of silent pleas,
Woven through the silent night,
Whispers carried on the breeze,
Heroes born without a fight.

The mind's canvas, painted bold,
With colors bright yet never seen,
Each brushstroke gently unfolds,
A world where stillness reigns supreme.

In corners where the shadows bend,
Consciousness begins to fade,
Yet in that space, the dreams extend,
A universe carefully laid.

So dive beneath the waking stream,
For what is real, and what's a thought?
Within the silent, endless dream,
The echoes of the mind are caught.

Echoes of Tomorrow's Dawn

Awake, the world begins to stir,
As whispers float on morning air,
Promises dance, a gentle blur,
With every light, a chance to care.

Beyond the hills where shadows play,
New dreams are born, fresh and bright,
Each heartbeat sings a brand new day,
Hope arises with the light.

In vibrant hues, the skies ignite,
A canvas stretched from earth to sky,
Each moment glows with pure delight,
As stars give way to sunlight's sigh.

The rhythms of the heart embrace,
Melodies of time unfold,
Through every challenge, every place,
A story waiting to be told.

So let the dawn fill all your dreams,
With echoes of the bright unknown,
Embrace the light, or so it seems,
For in this realm, you're not alone.

The Slumbering Vision

Beneath the veil of sleep's soft sigh,
A vision waits, both bold and bright,
In dreams where shadows flicker by,
The heart finds solace in the night.

Wrapped in the silence, tales are spun,
Of worlds where time dissolves away,
Each whispered thought, a silver sun,
Lighting paths that hearts will sway.

Through crystal skies and velvet seas,
The visions dance, they weave and play,
In the crevices of memories,
The slumbering dreams begin to sway.

While stars above in secrets glow,
A symphony of lives once lived,
In the quiet, soft and slow,
The dreams awaken, love is given.

So let the night embrace your mind,
For in the stillness, hope is sown,
With every journey, peace you'll find,
In slumber's arms, you are not alone.

Between Reality and Reverie

There lies a space of soft divide,
Where dreams and waking hours entwine,
A place where secrets softly glide,
And thoughts flow free like rich red wine.

In this realm where shadows meet,
The whispers of the heart confide,
With every pulse, the worlds compete,
For clarity where hopes abide.

Between the cracks of light and dark,
The echoes of a truth appear,
A symphony of life's sweet spark,
In every moment, drawing near.

Through winding paths of chance and fate,
The spirit dances, wild and free,
In wonderland, we recreate,
The ever-changing tapestry.

So venture forth in dreams' embrace,
Where stories blend and hearts can soar,
In every glance, each warm embrace,
The space between forevermore.

The Realm of Untold Stories

Hidden tales beneath the stars,
Whispers of time, she softly stirs.
In shadows where the silence grows,
Live dreams that only night bestows.

Voices echo from ancient lands,
With secrets woven in golden strands.
Their laughter dances with the breeze,
In every rustle of the trees.

In corners dark, where memories sleep,
The past is rich, its treasures deep.
A tapestry of hope and fears,
Unraveled softly, through the years.

With every turn, a path unfolds,
Of journeys long, and stories told.
In every heart, a spark ignites,
To guide us through the endless nights.

So come and wander, take a chance,
In this realm where shadows dance.
For in the quiet, secrets bide,
Awaiting those who choose to guide.

Reveries of the Restless Soul

In twilight hours where dreams reside,
A restless heart no longer hides.
It yearns to break the chains of night,
And soar beyond the morning light.

With every sigh, the winds reply,
They call to worlds where spirits fly.
In whispers soft, they weave a tune,
That echoes 'neath the velvet moon.

Across the seas of endless thought,
Life's tapestry is bravely wrought.
Each thread a hope, a thread a fear,
Entwined within the atmosphere.

The stars above, they paint a map,
Of all the dreams that laid to nap.
Awakened now, they shimmer bright,
In realms where day meets starry night.

With every heartbeat, courage blooms,
In gardens lush where freedom looms.
A symphony of souls in flight,
Together crafting boundless light.

Between the Past and Tomorrow

In the twilight of what has been,
And dreams that whisper, soft yet keen.
We walk the line, both thin and frail,
To find the truths in every tale.

Yesterday's shadows, memories sewn,
Teach us the seeds of courage grown.
In every step, a lesson lies,
A bridge to tomorrow, where hope flies.

The present sparkles, the now unfolds,
With every heartbeat, the future molds.
A dance of time, both swift and slow,
We learn from where the rivers flow.

Across the canvas of the skies,
Past dreams and wishes synch and rise.
In every ending, beginnings bloom,
An echo of what's yet to loom.

So walk with grace, with heart and mind,
In the space where life's entwined.
For in this journey, we ignite,
The flame of dreams that burns so bright.

The Awakening of Forgotten Wishes

In dreamers' hearts, where silence sleeps,
Lie gentle wishes, buried deep.
With every dawn, they start to stir,
Awakening hopes that softly purr.

Once tossed aside, like autumn leaves,
They long for winds, for gentle reprieves.
In every sigh, a promise breathes,
Of dreams once lost, now woven sheaves.

They rise like mist at break of day,
Each wish a note in night's ballet.
With courage pressed against despair,
They float like whispers in the air.

In glimmers bright, their light will shine,
Transforming fate, their paths align.
For in the heart of every soul,
Lies power waiting to console.

So let them soar, these forgotten dreams,
On currents high, where hope redeems.
In every moment, let us find,
The magic born from love entwined.

www.ingramcontent.com/pod-product-compliance
Ingram Content Group UK Ltd.
Pitfield, Milton Keynes, MK11 3LW, UK
UKHW030904221224
452712UK00007B/913